IT TAKES ONE

TO KNOW ONE

M. HELEN INGRAM

All scripture quotations are from the King James Version of the Bible unless otherwise indicated.

Printed in the United States of America

First printing May 2020

100 Fold Life Publishing

ISBN-13 - 978-1-7324084-4-9

It Takes One To Know One

Contents

ABSTRACT

ShemA Yisrael, Hear O Israel: the Lord our God is One Lord. Did ever people hear the voice of God speaking out of the midst of the fire, as thou hast heard, and live? Or hath God assayed to go and take him a nation from the midst of another nation, by temptations, by signs, by wonders, by war, by a mighty hand, by a stretched out arm, or by great terrors, according to all that the Lord your God did for you in Egypt before your eyes? Unto thee it was shewed, that thou mightest know that the Lord he is God: there is none else beside Him. Deut 4:33-35.

He was in the world, and the world was made by Him, and the world knew Him not. John 1:10.

And the LORD shall be king over all the earth: in that day shall there be one LORD, and his name One. Zech 14:9.

The ONE GOD is the truth. If His name is not to be believed on, then how unfathomable are His works which attest to his sovereignty or His Oneness. Through the many case studies and the analytical observations of their veracity, the conclusive inerrant evidence is that the God of Israel is the One God but *"It Takes One to Know One."*

M. Helen Ingram

＊ ＊ ＊

But from whence is my argument carved?
With what shall i accomplish its win?
O that i myself could only tell
Time delivers its now! And its when?
That through the utterance of my pen
He might some soul deliver
That which was fruit from some divine quiver
From the hellish pit of savagery and sin
Or perhaps at the strait gate enter in
By a sword that pierced the groaning heart
Its arrow between the joint and marrow
To save the soul but slay the sin

Poem by M. Ingram

＊ ＊ ＊

INTRODUCTION

The postmodern generation as in medieval Christendom and the first century or Apostolic church is confronted with varied belief systems relating to the life, death, burial and resurrection of Jesus Christ. There are differing terminologies, images and concepts associated with His salvific redemptive role. Persistent among the many discourses is the presentation of the contemporary significance of Christ and the revelation of just who He is. One question of today might be that of whether Jesus alone matches the identity of the Messiah from the Orthodox Jews' vantage point.

Another question presented is whether the biographies of Jesus withstand today's scrutiny in light of the information explosion or technological age? Is the Jesus of biblical history the same as the Jesus of today's faith and if so, why do we not as faith believers experience the same and greater works results as He did? Is He really the ONE or do we look for another as posed by John the Baptist? With the ever-growing acceptance of traditional taboos also nomenclatured as sin, should such losses or gains be considered as a civil right or a spiritual Armageddon? Have women usurped the power of the male dominated, patristically formulated foundation? Have the rappers of reality drowned out the woes of traditional formality? Have the pyrotechnics of musicality served as a substitution for the surreal meaningful spiritual experience?

The law of the Spirit of life in Christ has freed those who profess Christ as the Son of God from the law of sin and death. He is known to be Lord, Savior and Redeemer of souls from destruction. Yet there are others who question the saneness of believing that the soul has need of such salvaging. The various religions have their beliefs in either one god, no god, or as many gods as one believes is needed. Theism, Confucianism, and Buddhism profess no such thing as sin and deem such thought senseless. Daoism allows for as many or as few gods as one wills. Neither Judaism nor Islam describes "sin" or "salvation from sin" as its aim.

Only Christians seek salvation from sin. Jesus Christ as Lord and Savior paid the ultimate price of death on the cross for redemption and payment for the wages of sin. Yet even some professed believers question the security of salvation and whether the cost was fully paid at the cross or does there yet remain an "endurance to the end" test. Jesus Christ makes the case that He is the way, the truth, and the life. Given the fact that the truth is the correct response to any given question, Jesus is the answer. As the only begotten of the Father, He is full of grace and truth. *1 John 5:20* states "And we know that the Son of God is come, and hath given us an understanding, that we may know him that is true, and we are in Him that is true, even His Son Jesus Christ. This is the true God, and eternal life. And this is eternal life - that they may know me, the only true God, and Jesus Christ whom the Father has sent. *John 17:1-3*

Aside from knowing the only true God, a further question is derived concerning the aspects of knowledge as it relates to God. He that believeth on the Son of God hath the witness in himself and it is only by His Spirit that we can know Him. In the topic "It Takes One to Know One" the source and the writer Himself is One. The method utilized by the source Himself is the variant, is limitless, and unsearchable in the expression of Himself, His dominion, and His dominance. According to the written Word, every form of communiqué is available to Him because he is the One by whom all things consist.

PART I

HISTORICAL DEVELOPMENT OF CHRISTOLOGY

Christology is the branch of theology that deals with the identity of Jesus Christ especially in the area of relating to *His human and divine nature.*[i] Theology itself is not a Biblical term but rather a religious study. At its outset it was considered to be a study about religions or a specialized religious subject usually at a college or seminary. For this endeavor the branch of theology used is Christology. It stems from the Greek word Khristos (Christ) and (logia) meaning the study of. According to the Westminster Dictionary of Christian Theology, Christology is the critical inquiry into the significance of Christ for the Christian faith.

The Christocentric belief ascribes to the principle that Scripture is interpreted in relation to its center which is Christ and that Christ is the central person of the Bible. Therefore, Christology concerns itself with Jesus' nature and personhood in relation to God's nature and God's personhood. As such the details of his ministry, his acts and teachings are studied in order to gain an even greater knowledge of who Jesus is in his person and in his role as Savior. Jesus is the One in the Godhead or Trinity who came in the flesh, was crucified on the cross at Calvary, was buried, and was resurrected from the dead on the third day, ascended up to heaven and lives forever more, is yet interceding to the Father on behalf of those that are His and is seated at God the Father's right hand.

Scrutiny of deities, isms, tenets, belief systems et cetera sorely lack even the miniscule capacity to any claim of comparison to any degree of their godliness. Neither can they possess nor do they profess a heaven that declares their glory; or a firmament that sheweth forth their handiwork; or a day that uttereth speech, and a night that sheweth knowledge with no speech or language that does not hear their voice. *Psalms 19:1-3.*

ShemA Yisrael, Hear O Israel: The Lord our God is One Lord. There is One God and Father of all, who is above all, and through all, and in you all. There is one body, and one Spirit, even as ye are called in one hope of your calling. *Deuteronomy 6:4*; and *Ephesians 4:4¹*. The real sense of the word ShemA as recorded from the Hebrew alphabetic definitions is Hear, O Israel, *Jehovah (the ever existing One)* our *Elohim (our Triune God)* Jehovah "is One"· *Isaiah 44:8b* reads… Is there a God beside me? Yea, there

is no God; I *know not* any, writes the Omniscient
One. God further expostulates on the foolishness of
bowing down to worship a molten image (metallic or
stonecast sculpture) that is itself worthless, blind,
inanimate, and in whom there is no help.

The question posed to the Jewish people by God
was – "Did ever people hear the voice of God
speaking out of the midst of the fire, as thou hast
heard, and live? Or hath God assayed to go and take
him a nation from the midst of another nation, by
temptations, by signs, by wonders, by war, by a
mighty hand, by a stretched out arm, or by great
terrors, according to all that the Lord your God did
for you in Egypt before your eyes? Unto thee it was
shewed, that thou mightest *know* that the Lord he is
God: there is none else beside him." *Deut 4:33-35*.
The validity of the statement - It Takes One to
Know One" - is based on scripture as written in the
Canon of the Old and New Testament.

Questions continue steadfastly in Christendom
that have their roots in the origin of Christianity
itself. The dogmas discussed here in part have to do
with the Doctrines of God; of the Trinity, of the
Person of Christ, of Salvation, of the Body of Christ;

and of Eschatology. The ensuing explorations entail a look at the relational aspect as a believer in ONE God. It is this unity of faith of all believers and the cohesiveness of Christian thought and interpretation to which we continually direct our attention. The securing of this uniformity takes none other than the work of the Holy Spirit in His infinite wisdom.

It is by the sole enlightenment of the Word of God that one is compelled or constrained to pursue the higher calling as a chosen vessel of God. This is a time of recall to again stand at the crossroads and look. Ask for the ancient paths, ask where the good way is and walk in it - *John 6:16* - to perhaps in some manner or confession, lay claim to an even more joyful and steadfast claim to identification as it relates to the "ONE God

A bit of etymology – (study of origin and meaning of words) - is in order for the purpose of synchronization of the base meaning of the terms being utilized in the topic.

Theology:

(1) - The study of *theology* itself is easily broken down into two Greek words: *theos* (God) and *logos*

(word). Thus "*Theology*" is a study or discourse about God.

Scientia:

(1) - Science is in the Latin, *Scientia-* which is defined as knowledge

(2) - That which we know is truth that can never change.

Knowledge:

(1) - The state or fact of knowing

(2) - The sum or range of what has been perceived, discovered or learned.

(3) - Familiarity, awareness, or comprehension acquired by experience or study

(4) - Erudition

(5) – Specific information

(6) – Archaic Sexual intercourse

Knowing:

(1) –Possessing knowledge, intelligence, or comprehension

(2) – Possessing or exhibiting clever awareness and resourcefulness: shrewd

(3) – Deliberate

Know:

(1) – *Yada* in the Hebrew is a primitive root word meaning properly to ascertain by seeing. It is used in a variety of senses.

Figuratively – Representing by means of a figure, symbol or likeness

Literally – Following or representing the exact words of the original.

Euphemistically – Use of a word or phrase that is less expressive or direct but considered less distasteful, less offensive, et cetera than another.

Inferentially – A conclusion arrived at in logic by either induction or deduction.

Causatively – Producing an effect; causing.

Know:

(1) - To perceive directly with the senses or mind.

(2) - To believe to be true with absolute certainty.

(3) - To have a practical understanding of or thorough experience with.

(4) - To be subjected to: experience

(5) - a. To recognize (something) as being the same or something else previously known:

b. To be familiar with

(6)- To be able to distinguish, recognize

(7) – Archaic: Sexual intercourse

One:

(1) – The biblical numerical definition of the number One is self-revealing, self-proclaiming, and self-indicative of its significance

(2) – Symbol of unity

Oneness:

(1) – The fact or state of being unified or whole though comprised of two or more parts: the oneness of man and nature. <*Special Usage*) Identity or harmony with someone or something. A strong sense of oneness is felt with all things.

(2) – The fact or state of being one in number: belief in the oneness of God.

Revelation:

(1) – A surprising and previously unknown fact, especially one that is made known in a dramatic way

(2) – Something shown to us by God the Father. The divine or supernatural disclosure to human of something relating to human existence or the world.

THE DOCTRINE OF GOD

Doctrine is defined as that which is taught. Bible doctrine comes out of the word of God and is founded on the words of God. Hence the Doctrine of God teaches that: The Father is God:

Jesus of Nazareth is God
The Holy Spirit is God
God is One

In acceptance of the Word of Truth, such a one in order to be God is to be revered, worshipped, and adored. He is solitary in His majesty, unique in His excellency, peerless in His perfection, self-sustaining, self- existent, and self-satisfied.4 [ii] In God's application of teaching humankind about Himself, He approaches or introduces Himself through the following:

His very existence. – "I AM"
Making Himself known to man.
The names that he gives Himself.
His very essence as Deity.
His attributes.
His nature.
His manifold works.

The doctrine of God as seen from its Hebraic roots keeps the focus on an experiential and relational nature wherein the Hellenistic trend is intellectual and speculative in nature.5[iii]

According to Author Pink and the Biblical record, God's sovereignty is evidenced in the fact that He was under no constraint, no obligation, no necessity to create nor did it add to or subtract from his essence. Nor was He under any obligation to salvage His creation except that He was minded to according to His own good pleasure and His sovereign will. His independence in creation is His glory. The finiteness of man's comprehension often trumps the God of Scripture concerning His Being, his nature and His attributes and renders Him the *unknown* God to many.

A.W. Pink further suggests in his book *The Attributes of God* that the 20th century god of the pulpits trump the Supremacy of God with such rhetoric as can be called apostate Christendom. What or who he sees represented in the contemporary presentation is a God that is moved by sentimentality over principle, a God whose Omnipotence is being thwarted by Satan on every hand and changes His plans accordingly, a God whose power is restricted in proportion to man's "free will," a God whose atonement may be used if one feels so disposed to and presents the work of the Holy Spirit as an invitation to be responded to if it so pleases one to do so. He therefore deems the resemblance to the Holy Writ miniscule where God's supremacy and sovereignty is concerned.

E. W. Bullinger's exposition of the biblical meaning of the number one proves to be highly valuable and vital to gain a broadened depth of its definition. Though the following pages (16-18) are not verbatim, his revelational edge in his work is quite comprehensive and quite simplistic, and quite phenomenal. When the words *first, only, independent of, beginning, the only, et cetera* are used, *one is its synonym.* Bullinger notes that one in relation to God marks the *beginning.* God first is the voice of Scripture and there is only one first and hence man can never occupy God's space or be number one. No two objects can occupy the same space at the same time and God 's space never changes.

Redemption and salvation were *first* revealed by the word of God. It was His will that first proposed salvation and His power that accomplished it. Therefore, salvation is of the LORD. The *first* words written down accorded to Jesus was *Luke 2:49* "Wist ye not that I must be about my father's business?" Their *first* order of the words of Jesus written in the Bible bespeaks its *significance.* It was not until He finished his work that He said I have glorified Thee on the earth: I have finished the work that thou gavest Me to do." His *first* ministerial words have to do with "*It is written*" I have given them the words Thou gavest me. To those who have ears to hear, this says that the *beginning* and end of all ministry is the Word of God as it is written and that it is both the sum and substance of ministerial testimony. His testimony was not that of the price He paid for the anointing. He did not recount His missteps that caused Him to be obedient though he did learn obedience by the things He suffered. He did not conference with flesh for He knew what was in man. *Genesis 49:4* states that man is unstable as water, cease ye from man. ` God alone changes not as He is the Word.

The *first* book of Genesis shows Divine sovereignty and supremacy in Creation, in giving life, in sustaining life, and in His election in the calling of Abram, Isaac, and Jacob. The first commandment Hear, O Israel: the LORD our God is one LORD: thou shalt love the LORD thy God with all thy heart, and with all thy soul, and with all thy mind, and with all thy strength." This says *first* in order, *first* in time, and *first* in importance. "The Lord, our God, The Lord is One." The three, Father, Son, and Spirit is One.

There are two Hebrew words for the number "one" (Echad), *unus*; and (Yacheed), an only one, *unicus*. Yacheed means absolute unity, or uniqueness, an only one. It is used of the Lord Jesus as the only begotten Son but never of Jehovah, the Triune God. Echad is so used because it means a *compound unity* versus an *absolute unity.* No doubt surrounds the importance of this primary number according to the Greek lexicon. In all languages it is said to be the symbol of unity. As a cardinal number (prime, pivotal) it represents unity. As an ordinal number (indicating position in a series or order, *first)* it denotes primacy or state of being *first* or foremost. Unity, being indivisible and not made up of any other number, is therefore independent of all others. It is the source of all others. So, it is with Deity.

The *First Cause* is independent of all. All stand in need of Him and He needs no assistance from anyone. "One" excludes all differences, for there is no second with which it can either harmonize or conflict. God is One, is first, is the source, is the only, is independent, is the initiator, is the only true and living God, is one Lord, and is the great proclamation of all Scripture.[iv]

CHRISTOLOGY IN THE PATRISTIC PERIOD

The *Patristic Period* in the 1st century of church history saw concentrated effort being given to the doctrine of Christ. In light of Jesus' life, death, burial and resurrection as well as the notion of salvation and redemption, a new set of terms, images and ideas was needed as the existing structure available to church *paters* or fathers proved to be insufficient to express the progressing tide of events led to the beginnings of Christology. The miraculous healings of the sick, the raising of the dead, the opening of blind eyes, and the setting at liberty those who were imprisoned was met with differing degrees of skepticism.

Various approaches evolved from theological debates with subjects ranging from Jesus' divinity to his human aspect and his ministry. In the process of exploration for expression of the significance of Jesus of Nazareth, (the carpenter's son) as believers they were environmentally impacted regarding their belief system. The Jewish believers were convinced that their descent from Abraham guaranteed their spiritual deliverance whereas Jesus warned that true freedom came only through obedience to Him. The Jewish custom of burning large oil lamps in the temple area continuously symbolizing the fire that protected them in the wilderness was challenged by Jesus' claim to be the light of the world. Questions in the postmodern society remain one of truth whether relative to doctrinal issues or life in general. If once saved is one always saved? Can one be ye perfect? Do all roads lead to the One God? Have the names simply been changed but the One God is the same God? Or have the names been changed to protect the unwise and the unwilling? The presupposition that Jesus is God remains controversial aside from His redemptive and salvific roles. Again, only Christians seek salvation from sin.

THE DOCTRINE OF CHRIST

The Doctrine of Christ is the biblical teaching concerning the person and work of Jesus Christ. Jesus having appeared as the only begotten son in the fullness of time, and, having warned the disciples to beware the doctrine of the Pharisees and of the

Sadducees asked of them saying, "Whom do men say that I the *Son of man* am?'. Upon their response, Jesus asked a second question, "But whom say ye that I am?" Simon Peter answering said, "Thou art the Christ, the Son of the living God." Jesus responded to Peter, "Blessed art thou, Simon Barjona: for flesh and blood hath not revealed it unto thee, but my Father which is in heaven. And I say also unto thee, thou art Peter, and upon this rock I will build my church; and the gates of hell shall not prevail against it *(Mathew 16:13-18)*.

In another rendering we read that humankind has redemption through Jesus' shed blood, even the forgiveness of sins, that he is the image of the invisible God, the first born of every creature: by Him were all things created that are in heaven, and in earth, visible and invisible, whether they be thrones, or dominions, or principalities, or powers: they were all created by Him. It pleased the FATHER that in Him should all fullness dwell. *(Colossians1:14-10)*. We are all one in Christ Jesus if we are Christ's. The world belongs to Him. Jesus Himself prayed that those who did believe would be one in them, the

Godhead, that the world may believe that the Father sent Him.

In light of the divergence or convergence of doctrines, rituals, mythology, experience, law, and their effect on God's creation, samplings can be looked at from a *historical, chronological and or cultural* vantage point.   Truth enlightens the eyes of the understanding and increases knowledge in accordance with God's pleasure. Truth also serves as a catalyst for a deeper walk with God who Himself is both initiator and liberator. Within that liberation is the gift of eternal life. Now this is eternal life: that they may *know* you, the only true God, and Jesus Christ, whom you have sent - *John 17:1-3*. The concentration being given to the doctrine of the person of Christ began in the Eastern Church and the complex task confronted was that of development of a Christological scheme that would unify various hints, statements, images and models [v] found within the New Testament.

The first question centered on the divinity of Christ in light of the fact that Jesus was spoken of as a human being.

The exploration and explanation required searching out how Christ differed from other human beings. *Ebionitism*, which was rejected as being heretical, regarded Jesus as ordinary and simply the son of Joseph and Mary. The Jewish approach of Jesus being a prophet was considered inadequate. Doetism ("to seem or appear") which held that Christ was totally divine and his humanity was merely an appearance was shunned in favor of other viewpoints of the Apologists (Defender of one's belief against criticism) Justin Martyr and Origen. Justin Martyr's philosophy was that the Christian faith brought to fruition both classical Greek philosophy and Judaism, or both the Word *(logos)* and the Law *(nomos)*. He further stated that the Logos is known by Christian believers and pagan philosophers alike and that believers have the greater access to truth or the Logos through the mind and history. Apologist Origen's philosophy was the adoption of an illuminatist approach to revelation in which God's act of revelation is compared to being enlightened by the "rays of God" which are caused by the "light which is divine Logos." For Origen truth and salvation are available outside the Christian faith.

Still in process of exploration for expression of the significance of Jesus of Nazareth, there arose what is termed the *Arian controversy*[vi]. In the Arian belief system, the Son and the Father do not have the same essence (ousia). It states that the Son is a created being even though He is to be recognized as first and foremost in terms of origination and rank; and although the Son was the Creator of worlds, and must therefore have pre-existed before all time, there was nevertheless a time when the Son did not exist. Most fundamentally among Arian's belief was that Jesus Christ was not divine in any meaningful sense of the term although he is careful to argue that The Son is a perfect creature, yet not the same as one among other creatures; a begotten being, yet not the same as one among other begotten beings. To summarize his position again in reference to New Testament statements referring to Jesus as the "Son" according to Arius:

(1) The Son is a creature, who, like all other creatures, derives from the will of God.

(2) The term "Son of God" is a metaphor, an honorific term intended to underscore the rank of the Son among other creatures. It does not imply that Father and Son share the same being or status.

(3) The status of the Son is itself a consequence not of the nature of the Son, but of the will of the Father. Therefore, Arius draws an absolute distinction between God and the created order. He saw God as being both transcendent and immutable.

The question in Arius' mind was how can an immutable God be changeable, capable of moral development, subject to pain, fear, grief, and weariness. To him it seemed heretical. God's utter transcendence and inaccessibility precludes God from being known by any creature and the Son is dependent upon the grace of God to perform whatever function has been ascribed to him. The strict Greek philosophical monotheisms of his age shunned the idea of the incarnation as being consistent with the changeableness and transcendency of God.

With such a strong rational approach to the identity of Jesus Christ, why the attraction of such vigorous criticism?

Athanasius of Alexandria's critique of Arius is that he destroyed the internal coherence of the Christian faith, rupturing the close connection between Christian belief and worship. Having as his foundation that it is only God who can save and that God alone can break the power of sin, and bring humanity to eternal life, he counters Arianism with the fact that no creature can redeem another creature. He states that according to Arius, Jesus Christ is a creature and therefore according to Arius, Jesus Christ cannot redeem humanity. Since Arius was committed to the idea that Christ was the Savior, Athanius' point was that Arius had made the claim incoherent. Athanasius further pointed out that Christians worship and pray to Jesus Christ and if Jesus was a creature then they had lapsed into idolatry which is explicitly prohibited.

The debates ended with the judicious compromise in the use of two terms describing the relation of the Father to the Son. – *homoiousios*, (of like substance) and *homoousios*, (of the same substance). The Niceno –Constantinopolitan Creed of 381 declared that Christ was "of the same substance." This affirmation is widely regarded as a benchmark of Christological orthodoxy with all mainstream Christian churches whether Protestant, Catholic, or Orthodox.[vii]

The Nicene Creed:

I Believe in one God, the Father Almighty,
maker of heaven and earth, and of all things visible and invisible.
I believe in one Lord Jesus Christ, the only Son of God,
begotten of the Father before all ages, God from God,
Light from Light, true God from true God, begotten not made,
of one Being with the Father; through Him all things were made.
For us and for our salvation He came down from heaven, and was
incarnate from the Holy Spirit and the Virgin Mary, and was made man.
For our sake He was crucified under Pontius Pilate; He suffered death
and was buried. On the third day He rose again in accordance with the
Scriptures; He ascended into heaven and is seated at the right hand of the
Father. He shall come again in glory to judge the living and the dead, and
His kingdom will have no end. I believe in the Holy Spirit, the Lord, the
Giver of life, who proceeds from the Father [and the Son], who with the
Father and the Son is worshipped and glorified, who has spoken through
the prophets. I believe in one, holy, catholic, and apostolic Church. I
acknowledge one baptism for the forgiveness of sins. I look for the
resurrection of the dead, and the life of the world to come. Amen.

The *Alexandrian School* to which Athanasius is to be assigned focuses sharply on the significance of Christ as savior (Greek: soter) of humanity. Christology gives expression to what this soteriological insight implies. In the main, God became human in order that humanity might become divine. The writers put emphasis on the idea of the Logos assuming human or taking human nature upon itself as in the incarnation of the Son of God as opposed to the Old Testament where the Logos was dwelling within humanity. The Word or flesh assumed the human nature of flesh in order to redeem it.

The question then raised was the relation of the divinity and humanity of Christ.

The Alexandrian School taught that the Logos existed "without flesh" before its union with human nature and after that union, there is only one nature in that the Logos joined human nature to itself. The *Antiochene School* on the other hand is more receptive to the idea of two natures within Christ. It deemed in declaring the Word was made to be incarnate and made human does not necessarily mean that there was any change in the nature of the Word when it became flesh or that it was transformed into an entire human being. It held rather, that the Word in an indescribable and inconceivable manner, united personally to Himself flesh endowed with a rational soul, and thus became a human being and was called the Son of man. This then led to the question of what kind of human nature had been assumed? Was human nature assumed in its entirety by the Logos?

Apollinarius of Laodicea expressed reservations about the increasingly widespread belief that the Logos assumed human nature in its entirety because it implied that the Logos was contaminated by the weaknesses of human nature. Was not the human mind the source of sin and rebellion against God? His argument therefore was that in Christ, a purely human mind and soul were replaced by a divine mind and soul; and the divine energy fulfills the role of the animating soul and of the human mind in Christ.

The human nature of Christ is thus incomplete. This idea proved to be appalling to many colleagues while attractive to others. The soteriological implications were shocking to some, especially Gregory of Naziannus (329-89) in that it denied the assumption of human nature in its totality at the incarnation. Gregory's idea was that what has not been assumed has not been healed; it is what is united to his divinity that is saved. So, he admonishes that total salvation go not unclaimed nor that the Savior have mere appearance of humanity. The Antiochene response to criticism was that the complete unit of Christ is not inconsistent with his possessing two natures - Divine and human. The summarization therefore of the school of Alexandria: Logos assumes a general human nature. Antioch: Logos assumes a specific human nature.

The question that then ensued was how are the human and divine natures related?

Whereas the Alexandrian position is one where the Logos assumes a general human nature, the Antiochene school of thought is that the natures remain distinct in their respective existence and remain in conjoined compartments (hypostasis) that do not detach because the one who was assumed is united in honor and glory with the one who assumed according to the will of the one who assumed him.

The writer by the name of Theodore seems to regard the hypostatic union as a conjunction according to the will of the parties involved such as in a marriage contract.

The "*communication of attributes*" was of great concern to the patristic writers who focused on the question of this approach in coming to certain Christological conclusions. The propositions that Jesus is fully human and that Jesus is fully divine gained popular acceptance. The argument was that if these two statements were simultaneously true then what was true of the humanity of Jesus must also be true of his divinity and vice versa. Out of such dialogue arose the *Nestorian Controversy* wherein he questioned the seeming denial of the humanity of Christ.[viii] However Martin Luther had no hesitation in using this approach. According to Luther the lines read as thus: Jesus Christ was crucified. Jesus is God. Therefore, God was crucified. This line of thinking some regarded as a radical application of the "communication of attributes."

A decisive turning point was made in the history of Christian thought and its development on the basis of the studies of the German liberal Protestant scholar, Adolph von Harnack (1851-1930). He emphatically argued that the transition of the gospel from its original *Palestinian milieu* dominated by Hebraic modes of thought and rationality to a *Hellenic milieu* characterized by radically different modes of thinking led to the attempt to conceptualize and give metaphysical substance to the significance of Jesus. Harnack argues that dogma owes or renders nothing to the teaching of Jesus Christ or to primitive Christianity in its original Palestinian context. Instead he credits dogma to a specific historical location characterized by Hellenistic modes of thoughts and patterns of discourse, and consequently its formulation.

To Harnack, the gospel is nothing other than Jesus Christ himself and He is not one of its elements. He states that Jesus is the personal realization and power of the gospel and that He is Christianity. In his work *The History of Dogma (1894-8)*, Harnack illustrates the trend to conceptualize and give metaphysical substance to the significance of Jesus with reference to Gnosticism, the Apologist, and the Logos-Christology of Origen. He likens the view to a chronic degenerative illness. He notes a shift from soteriology and the personal impact of Jesus to a speculative metaphysical retreat to the abstract. He makes three historical observations in support of his thesis as follows:

(1) A Christology (that is, a doctrine of the person of Christ) is not part of the proclamation of Jesus of Nazareth. Jesus' own message does not include a Christology, in that it includes no self-referring affirmations. It is this point that underlies Harnack's famous-often totally misunderstood-statement that "the gospel, as Jesus proclaimed it, has to do with the Father only and not the Son."

(2) In the history of Christian thought, a concern with Christology was both chronologically and conceptually posterior to a concern with soteriology.

(3) The concern with Christology arose within a Hellenistic culture, which echoed a characteristic Greek concern for abstract speculation.

His observations prompted a renewed interest in the study of the patristic period with the end result being a warning of the danger in regarding the patristic writers as having authoritative status in matters of doctrine. One such writer was Irenaeus of

Lyons, Bishop and Father of Church was said to
have heard and seen the holy Bishop Polycarp at
Smyrna who was a disciple of St. John. He was priest
during the persecution of Marcus Aurelius and was
sent to Rome by his peers on behalf of those
imprisoned for the Faith. He wrote in Greek and his
works secured him an exceptional place in Christian
writings. His topics were mostly against Gnosticism
which was considered a heretical teaching that
embraced among its tenets that Jesus did not die.

CHRISTOLOGY IN THE MEDIEVAL PERIOD

During the medieval period (c.700- c1500), there was systematic exploration of logical and philosophical aspects of most areas of theology including Christology. The question of this era was posed in this fashion.

Was the incarnation dependent on Adam's fall or would it have happened anyway?

The prevalent understanding was that humanity fell from grace and required restoration which in turn required incarnation of the Son of God and his saving work on the cross. Therefore, if humanity had not sinned there would have been no need for the incarnation. However, Honorius of Autun, a theologian over the period of 1106-35, argued from another vantage point. His view was that the incarnation was not ordained as a remedy for human sin but in order to secure the divinization of humanity.

A similar view is found in the writings of the Benedictine theologian Rupert of Deutz (c1075-1129) who also argued that the incarnation was the result of God's wish to dwell among his people and therefore should be seen as a climax of the work of creation rather than a reaction to human sin. Thomas Aquinas (c1225-1274) is seen as the adjudicator of this debate. He realized the highly speculative nature of the question and resorted to the Holy Scripture wherein is God's divine will and His revelation. He stated therefore since the sin of the first being is described as the cause of the incarnation throughout Holy Scripture, it is more in accordance to say that incarnation was ordained as a remedy for sin while simultaneously acknowledging God's limitless power.

Then what is the relation between the person of Christ and the work of Christ?

Older works of Christian theology often draw a sharp distinction between "the person of Christ" or Christology, on the one hand and "soteriology," or salvation on the other. Among the considerations which led to this development are the following:

(1) The philosopher Immanuel Kant (1724-1804) drew a distinction between the "thing in itself" and the human perception of "this thing." He argues that one cannot know things directly but only insofar as one can perceive them or apprehend their impact. Theologically, the implication is that the identity of Jesus is known through his impact upon one or said otherwise, the person of Christ becomes known through his work. This he deemed as a fundamental link between Christology and Soteriology. Modern Christology features this characteristic that the divine human person of Christ and his redemptive work are not separate and distinct as was taught in medieval Scholastic theology. Schleiermacher calls them two sides of the same coin. Charles Gore (1853-1932) pointed out that inadequate conception of Christ's person go hand in hand with inadequate conceptions of what human nature wants. The Nestorian conception of Christ qualifies Christ for being an example of what man can do, and into what wonderful union with God can be assumed if man is holy enough.

(2) The increasing realization of the affinities between functional and ontological Christologies – that is functionally- the work of Christ and ontologically-his identity or being. Athanasius is one of the earliest Christian writers to make this connection clear. Only God can save, he asserts. Yet Christ is Savior. The question is, "What does this statement concerning the function of Christ tell us about his identity? "If Jesus Christ is capable of functioning as Savior, who must he be? Christology and Soteriology are thus seen as two sides of the same coin and not independent of each other. Christological models have the task of clarification of relationship between human and divine elements in the person of Jesus Christ. The Council of Chalcedon (451) represents Christ as a human figure with divine authority.

M. Helen Ingram

Council of Chalcedon 451 Creed:

We, then, following the holy Fathers, all with one consent, teach men to confess one and the same Son, our Lord Jesus Christ, the same perfect in Godhead and also perfect in manhood; truly God and truly man, of a reasonable soul and body; consubstantial with the Father according to the Godhead, and consubstantial with us according to the Manhood; in all things like unto us, without sin; begotten before all ages of the Father according to the Godhead, and in these latter days, for us and for our salvation, born of the Virgin Mary, the Mother of God, according to the Manhood; one and the same Christ, Son, Lord, only begotten, to be acknowledged in two natures, unconfusedly, unchangeably, indivisibly, inseparably; the distinction of natures being by no means taken away by the union, but rather the property of each nature being preserved, and concurring in one Person and one Subsistence, not parted or divided into two persons, but one and the same Son, and only begotten, God the Word, the Lord Jesus Christ; as the prophets from the beginning have declared concerning Him, and the Lord Jesus Christ Himself has taught us, and the Creed of the holy Fathers has handed down to us.

THE DOCTRINE OF SOTERIOLOGY

Soteriology (soteria, salvation, *logos,* discourse) as the other side of the coin of Christology refers to the study of the doctrine concerning salvation. It includes God's purpose to save, the Person and work of the Redeemer and the application of redemption by the work of the Holy Spirit. The six foundational principles on which the doctrine of Soteriology rests are as follows:

(1) God's rule is sovereign.

(2) God as Creator, Ruler, and Savior underlies all the provisions of salvation.

(3) Man has responsibility to his Creator because he has the capacity for good and bad.

(4) The Law of God requires perfect obedience.

(5) The Covenant of Works expresses God's will and man's obligation.

(6) God as a perfect Being cannot require less than perfection in His Moral Law

Under the umbrella of Soteriology there are covenants, decrees or views that have incorporated doctrines specific to their individual attribute such as election, predestination, and atonement. The term salvation can be used in either a religious or secular manner. Regeneration is the action of the Spirit of God in the soul of the sinner, breeding by supernatural birth the very nature and life of God into his soul, literally making him a child of God, imparting unto him a new mature creation in God's own likeness in righteousness and true holiness.[ix] This new nature being the nature of God and the residence of the Spirit of God in the soul is the very life of God Himself. This seed of God in the soul cannot sin. The fact that the Spirit of God alone is able to regenerate the soul is clearly seen when the nature of regeneration is seen. The sinner cannot bore himself again as neither can a baby. Christ further states that one is born not of man, nor the will of man but of God. The Holy Spirit is the direct agent breeding the nature and life of God into the soul.

THE DOCTRINE OF THE CHURCH

What is the historical verdict of history? Can the biographies survive the scrutiny? Was the evidence credible? Has it been reliably preserved?

The area of Christian theology which deals with the doctrine of the church is usually referred to as ecclesiology (Greek: ekklesia, "church") The early church has its beginnings set in the Book of Acts under Lucan authorship. ˣ Luke is said to be Greek in nationality, a physician by trade, a native of Antioch, Syria, never married, and died in Boetia at the age of eighty-four. The Book of Acts was written in the latter half of the first century wherein Luke was known for his accuracy in the presentation of summarizations of messages though not in verbatim format.   The Holy Spirit is acknowledged to be prominent in providing the miraculous power, the wisdom and the guidance. Luke traced the development of the Gospel from Jerusalem to Rome although his coverage is selective rather than comprehensive, omitting the Egyptian and Arabian Christians.[xi].

The textual integrity of Acts as written by Luke has been preserved in essentially two forms. The uncial (A style of writing characterized by somewhat rounded capital letters) manuscripts of Sinaitic and Vaticanus are foundational for all Modern Greek texts of Acts as well as the English translations. The second text form is in the uncial manuscript Beza (known by the text symbol D), is approximately10 percent longer and due to geographic origin is considered Western. These additions contained in the Besae texts are secondary and usually ethical in nature. Mainly, the additions are to remove grammatical difficulties, to clarify ambiguities, to add references to Christ, and to insert historical details.

The contents of Acts provide a short summary of his Gospel before going forth with story of the church. Luke begins Acts with emphasizing:

(1) the commandments given to the disciples,

(2) the genuineness of the resurrection appearances, and (3) the promised coming of the Holy Spirit. He contrasts what Jesus *Himself* began to do and teach over against what Jesus does and

teaches through the apostles and other witnesses. Even the usage of the term baptized with the Holy Spirit described as a pouring out of the Spirit by God on his people at Pentecost is contrasted in *1 Corinthians 12:13* wherein it refers to an experience at conversion by which all believers are transformed by the presence of God and united into the body with Christ – for by one Spirit are we all baptized into one body, and have all been made to drink into one Spirit.

The Ascension was the visible act wherein Jesus received exaltation to God's right hand and in this upward movement showed the transcendence of God. The reality side of the Ascension pointed to the hope of Jesus' return as proclaimed by the two men in white apparel which said to the Galileans '...this same Jesus which is taken up from you into heaven, shall so come in like manner as ye have seen him go up into heaven. This same Jesus that had been born of a virgin in Bethlehem, the city of David. This same Jesus who was the promised Seed of Abraham as was written by the law and the prophets. This same Jesus who was from Nazareth and the son of a carpenter. This same Jesus, who in response to John's question of 'is He the one or should we look for another was 'Go and show John again those things which ye do hear and see; the blind receive their sight, and the lame walk, the lepers are cleansed, and the deaf hear, the dead are raised up, and the poor have the gospel preached to them, and blessed is he whosoever shall not be offended in Me. This same Jesus whose visage was marred more than any man, who shed His innocent blood for the redemption of mankind, delivered to the Gentiles, mocked, spitefully entreated, spitted upon, scourged, put to death on a cross at calvary, spent three days and three nights in the lower part of the earth having spoiled principalities and powers, made a shew of them openly, triumphing over them. This same Jesus, who on the third day rose from the grave with the keys of death and hell in His hands, showed Himself alive after His passion by many infallible proofs, being seen of them forty days, speaking of the things pertaining to the kingdom. This same Jesus that spoke to them that it was expedient for them that He go away; for if He go not away, the Comforter will not come unto you; but if I depart, I will send him unto you. Jesus, being assembled together with the apostles along with others totaling 120, commanded them that they should not depart from Jerusalem, but wait for the promise of the Father, which they had heard of Him. For John truly baptized with water; but ye shall be baptized with the Holy Spirit not many days hence.

When the day of Pentecost was fully come, they were all with one accord in one place and SUDDENLY, there came a sound from heaven as of a rushing mighty wind, and it filled all the house where they were sitting. And there appeared unto them cloven tongues like as of fire, and it sat upon each of them, and they were all filled with the Holy Spirit and began to speak with other tongues, as the Spirit gave them utterance. And there were dwelling at Jerusalem Jews, devout men, out of every nation under heaven and when it was noised abroad, the multitude came together, and were confounded, because that every man heard them speak in own language, and they were all amazed and marveled, saying to one another, Behold, are not all these which speak Galileans? And how hear we every man in our own tongue, wherein we were born? Parthians, Cretes, and Arabians, we do hear them speak in our tongues the wonderful works of God. And they were all amazed, and were in doubt, saying to one another, What meaneth this? Others mocking said, "These men are full of new wine. But Peter, standing up with the eleven, lifted up his voice, and said unto them: the sun shall be turned into Ye men of Judea, and all ye that dwell in Jerusalem, be this known unto you, and hearken to my words: for these are not drunk as ye suppose, seeing it is but the third hour of the day. But this is that which was spoken by the prophet Joel, "And it shall come to pass in the last days saith God, I will pour out of my Spirit upon all flesh; and your young men shall see visions, and your old men shall dream dreams, and on my servants and on my handmaidens I will pour out in those days of my Spirit; and they shall prophesy; *Acts 2:1-16*. Henceforth, we know Him no more after the flesh, yea; though we have known Christ Jesus after the flesh, yet now, henceforth, we know him no more.

During the intermittent period between His Acension and His second coming, the disciples are to spread the gospel, not to only the Jew or the lost sheep of Israel –Mathew 10:6- "but the LORD chose Saul as the vessel to him to bear His name to

the Gentiles. Another contrast given was casting of
lots (in this case for Matthias as Judas' replacement)
as a proper procedure before Pentecost whereas now
believers are led by the Spirit of God. Pentecost was
a Feast day in which the wheat harvest was celebrated
by the Jews also became for them a traditional day on
which Moses received the law at Sinai[xii] and would
clash over the relationship of grace and law; and
bringing of the gospel to the Gentiles and
abandoning of strict Jewish legalism.

Peter having recounted the death, burial and
resurrection and ascension of Jesus, pointing out His
Messiahship and Lordship, the Jews' immediate
response was, "What shall we do?" Peter urged them
to repent and submit to baptism as a sign of faith in
Christ. The Apostle Peter's healing of the lame man
was attributed to the power of the resurrected Christ.
This doctrine of resurrection was denied by the
Jewish religious Sect of the Sadducees. Peter along
with John denied their exhortation to cease preaching
in the name of Jesus and affirmed their course of
action to continue to preach what they had seen and
heard. As Christians, they demonstrated their love
for God, their unity, and their love for one another

by generous sharing (p 293). Church growth occurred rapidly. Three thousand (3000) souls were added to the Church on the day of Pentecost.

The Hebraists (primarily Semitic speaking Jews) and Hellenists (primarily Greek speaking Jews) were among those responding to the message of the gospel. By the leading of the Holy Spirit seven men were selected principally from the Greek speaking element of the church to handle the responsibility of food distribution thus leaving the apostles free to devote their full attention to prayer and to preaching the gospel. This action resulted in the continued spread of the gospel.

Stephen was one of the original seven who was found to be full of the Holy Spirit and was adamant about not limiting his ministry to caring for the needy. The vigorousness with which he preached led to the charges against him of teaching that Jesus would destroy the temple and change the customs of Moses. Stephen's response was to remind the Jews that they had not only rejected and disobeyed Moses and those whom God had raised up to deliver them, and that they themselves had fallen into idolatry as had their predecessors and were assuming that God inhabited their temple. This reponse led to his being stoned by the audience. This martyrdom of Stephen led to persecution against the Jerusalem church and all except the apostles fled from the city.

Hence, we see again the spreading of the gospel from Jerusalem to Samaria where the widespread ministry of Philip resulted in many being converted to Christianity and was accompanied by obvious miraculous signs and moral changes in the Samaritans. Simon the Sorcerer was one of those converts that professed a genuine belief in Christianity. However, his questionable act of proposing to pay for the Holy Spirit cast doubt on whether his motive was more attributable to his interest in retaining his profitable financial control over the people rather than his genuine belief in Christ. In Samaria, the bestowal of the Holy Spirit by Philips' laying on of hand was delayed from the time of conversion and it served two purposes:[xiii]

(1) A delay in giving the Spirit to the Samaritans gave the Jews who saw the physical evidence of the Spirit's coming, confidence that even outcast Samaritans could be converted.

(2) The bestowal of the Spirit to the Samaritans by the hands of Jewish Christians provided a foundation for unity between believers who might have otherwise viewed one another with suspicion (pgs 294-295).

Although not allowed to enter the temple as a Eunuch, there had now come a better promise of hope for eunuchs. Under God's direction, Philip traveled from Jerusalem to Gaza and secondly, he compelled Philip to approach the eunuch's chariot where he heard him reading aloud from the Book of Isaiah. Upon inquiry concerning comprehension of what was being read, the invitation was extended to Philip to join him and in so doing, Philip declared the story of Jesus to the attentive official. Having approached a body of water, the eunuch requested baptism whereupon Philip baptized by immersion the new believer as they came up from the water; the Holy Spirit snatched Philip away from the eunuch. This has been suggested as translation by some and by others it may simply have meant that Philip was led to move to another place of ministry.

This story is considered to have incredible value in revealing the leadership of the Holy Spirit in the missionary expansion of the early church. It also provides evidence of the power of the prophetic Scriptures in witnessing to the work of Jesus. The church father Irenaeus stated that the converted eunuch became a missionary to his own people, but there are no records of the Ethiopian church prior to the fourth century.

The significance of Paul's conversion is underscored by the fact that its narration is rendered three different times in the Book of Acts. Paul desired of the high priest letters to Damascus to the synagogues, that if he found any of this way, whether they were men or women, he might bring them bound unto Jerusalem. The Christians were mainly Jewish converts from Judaism. As Paul neared Damascus, he was suddenly surrounded by an intensely bright light. He heard a voice speaking to him, but those traveling with him stood speechless, hearing a voice, but seeing no man. Due to the sight, sound, and subsequent blinding of Paul, his companions led him by the hand into Damascus where he did neither eat nor drink for three days. God instructed Ananias, a devout Jewish Christian, to inquire in the house of Judas for one called Saul of

Tarsus, that he might receive his sight and be filled with the Holy Spirit.

It was Saul of Tarsus, renamed Paul, by trade a tentmaker, a zealot for Judaism, a very strict Pharisee, educated under Gamaliel, a member of the Sanhedrin Council, consenter to the stoning death of Stephen; who God, in response to Ananias ' recall to God, the much evil he (Paul) had done to the saints at Jerusalem said, "Go thy way: for he is a chosen vessel unto me, to bear my name before the Gentiles, and kings, and the children of Israel: for I must shew him how great things he must suffer for my name's sake. *Acts 9:13-15*

When it pleased God who separated Paul from his mother's womb and called him by His grace, to reveal His Son in him that he might preach Him among the heathen, immediately he conferred not with flesh and blood, nor with the disciples at Jerusalem. *Galatians 1:11-17* reads as stated by Paul, the apostle to the Gentiles by the will of God, I certify you brethren, that the gospel which was preached of me is not after man. For I neither received it of man, neither was I taught it, but by the revelation of Jesus Christ, For ye have heard of my conversation in time past in the Jew's religion how that beyond measure I persecuted the church of God, and wasted it: and profited in the Jew's religion above many my equals in mine own nation, being more exceedingly zealous of the traditions of my fathers. But when it pleased God, who separated me from my mother's womb, and called me by his grace, to reveal his Son in me, that I might preach him among the heathen; immediately I conferred not with flesh and blood; neither went I up to Jerusalem to them which were apostles before me; but I went into Arabia, and returned again unto Damascus.

He that had persecuted in times past now preached the faith which once he destroyed, preaching that Jesus was the Son of God and strongly admonished that if he or an angel from heaven preach any other gospel, let him be accursed. He continually returned to Damascus in the face of Jewish opposition, which for his better interest, he left the city for Jerusalem. In Jerusalem, the apostles still held doubt as to the veracity of Paul's conversion and his preaching led to such opposition that he was sent away by the disciples to his native Tarsus. Paul is next heard of when Barnabas seeks him out and brings him to Antioch. *Acts 11:25.*

At this interval, Luke records the miraculous activity of Peter proving that God had performed mighty works through Peter in the period leading up to his ministry among the Gentiles and that he had not fallen into spiritual compromise as he shared the gospel with the Gentiles. Peter exhibited that he had outgrown Jewish legalism by residing with Simon the tanner in Joppa as tanners were ceremonially unclean because of their contact with dead animals and were avoided by most scrupulous Jews. Peter was convinced that contact with Gentiles was acceptable to God due to a *God given vision.* He recounted to the apostles and his brethren that he was in the city of Joppa praying and, in a trance, he saw a vision of a white sheet let down from heaven by four corners. It contained fourfooted beasts, wild beasts, and creeping things, and fowls of the air, of which he was told to "Arise, slay, and eat." These were ceremonially impure animals of which God commanded him to kill and eat.

The vision convinced Peter that God had nullified the Mosaic dietary restriction. The Gentile failure to observe these restrictions had been a chief reason for the reluctance of Jews to fellowship with Gentiles. Abolishing these restrictions opened the way for fellowship of Jewish Christians with Gentiles. Peter grasped this truth and followed divine leadership to preach in the home of Cornelius, a Roman centurion. Peter's sermon to the Gentiles is an excellent example of C.H. Dodd's definition of the *kerygma* or preaching of the gospel. In this sermon Peter emphasized God's acceptance of people from every nation. Before the conclusion of Peter's message God poured out the Holy Spirit on the largely Gentile audience.

The presence of the Spirit was demonstrated by the physical evidence of *glossalalia* (speaking in tongues) which prompted Peter to declare that the Gentiles were to be baptized in the name of the Lord. Several days later the Jewish Christians in Jerusalem accused Peter of unlawful assembly with the Gentiles. In defense of his actions Peter recounted God's revelation in Cornelius' house. He wisely had taken with him six other Jewish Christian believers. Their combined testimonies of God's work convinced most of the audience that God had granted salvation to the Gentiles. There would be other clashes in the future over the *relationship of Christianity to the law,* but this incident provided a first step toward bringing the gospel to the Gentiles and abandoning strict Jewish legalism.

Just as the Son of God in Paul was revealed to him when it pleased God, God also revealed mysteries (something unknown except by divine revelation) to Paul that, which from the beginning of the world had been hid in God who created all things by Jesus Christ. *Eph 3:9b*   He states in *Romans 11:25* in regard to Israel's blindness and lawlessness, "I would not, brethren, that ye should be ignorant of this mystery, lest ye should be wise in your own conceits; that "blindness" in part is happened to Israel, until the fullness of the Gentiles be come in. The Israelites knew not their hour of visitation, *Luke 19:44. Deuteronomy 29:29* states, 'The secret things belong unto the LORD our God: but those things which are revealed belong unto us and to our children forever, that we may do all the works of this law. In *Colossians 1:25* in regard to the body of Christ "Whereof I am made a minister, according to the dispensation of God which is given to me for you, to fulfill the word of God; Even the mystery which hath been hid from ages and from generations, but is now made manifest to the saints: To whom God would make known what is the riches of the glory of this mystery among the Gentiles; which is Christ in you, the hope of glory...

In *Ephesians 3:4-9* we read concerning believers "Whereby, when ye read, ye may understand my knowledge in the mystery of Christ) which in other ages was not made known to the sons of men, as it is now revealed unto His holy apostles and prophets by the Holy Spirit; that the Gentiles should be fellow heirs, and of the same body, and partakers of his promise in Christ by the gospel: whereof I was made a minister, according to the gift of the grace of God given unto me by the effectual working of His power, unto me, who am less than the least of all saints, is this grace given, that I should preach among the Gentiles the unsearchable riches of Christ; and to make all men see what is the fellowship of the mystery, which from the beginning of the world hath been hid in God, who created all things by Jesus Christ. *1 Timothy 3:16* tells us concerning Christ's incarnation, that "Without controversy, great is the mystery of godliness; God was manifest in the flesh, justified in the Spirit, seen of angels, preached unto the Gentiles, believed on in the world, and received up into glory.

Concerning the will of God, we read (For the children being not yet born, neither having done any good or evil, that the purpose of God according to election might stand, not of works, but of Him that calleth. It was said unto her (Rebecca), the elder shall serve the younger, As it is written, "Jacob have I loved, but Esau have I hated. What shall we say then? Is there unrighteous with God? God forbid, for He saith unto Moses, I will have mercy on whom I will have mercy, and I will have compassion on whom I will have compassion. So, then it is not of him that willeth, nor of him that runneth, but of God that showeth mercy. For the scripture saith unto Pharaoh, even for the same purpose have I raised thee up, that I might show my power in thee, and that my name might be declared throughout all the earth.

Therefore, hath He mercy on whom He will have mercy, and whom He will he hardeneth. Thou will then say unto me, Why doth He yet find fault?

For who hath resisted His will? Nay but, O man, who art thou that repliest against God? Shall the thing formed say to him that formed it, Why hast thy made me thus? Hath not the potter power over the clay, of the same lump to make one vessel unto honor and another to dishonor? What if God, willing to show His wrath, and to make His power known, endured with such long-suffering the vessels of wrath fitted to destruction: and that He might make known the riches of His glory on the vessels of mercy, which He had afore prepared unto glory *Romans 9:11-23*.

Concerning the nature of God *Colossians 2:2* we read "That their hearts might be comforted, being knit together in love, and unto all the riches of the full assurance of understanding, to the acknowledgment of the mystery of God, and of the Father, and of Christ…..in whom are hid all the treasures of wisdom and knowledge. Concerning Christian faith that indwells we read in *1 Timothy 3:9* "Holding the mystery of the faith in a pure conscience. Before faith came, we were kept under the law, shut up unto the faith which should afterwards be revealed. Scripture concluded all under sin that the promise by faith of Jesus Christ might be given to them that believe.

Concerning iniquity which is the depth of sin *2 Thessalonians 2:7* reads, "For the mystery of iniquity doth already work: only He who now letteth will let, until He be taken out of the way. Concerning the translation of saints, *1 Corinthians 15:51* reads "Behold, I shew you a mystery; we shall not all sleep, but we shall all be changed. In a moment, in the twinkling of an eye, at the last trump: for the trumpet shall sound, and the dead shall be raised incorruptible, and we shall be changed. This grace was given by God to Paul to preach among the Gentiles the unsearchable riches of Christ: and to make all men see (in Christ there is neither Greek/Gentile nor Jew, circumcision nor uncircumcision, Barbarian, Scythian, bond nor free: but Christ is all in all. *Col 3:11*) what is the fellowship of the mystery, which from the beginning of the world hath been hid in God, who created all things by Jesus Christ….to the intent that now unto the principalities and powers in heavenly places might be known by the church the manifold wisdom of God.

Again, even the mystery which hath been hid
from ages and from generations, but now is made
manifest to His saints: to whom God would make
known what is the riches of the glory of this mystery
among the Gentiles; Christ in you, the hope of glory.
He goes on to say in *2 Corinthians 5:17* that if any
man be in Christ, he is a new creation: old things are
passed away; behold, all things are become new. The
middle wall of partition was broken down through
the blood of Jesus Christ having abolished in his
flesh the enmity due to the law and commandments.
For by one Spirit are we all baptized into one body,
whether we be Jew or Gentile, whether we be bond
or free, and have been all made to drink into one
Spirit.

Epicureanism and Stoicism (*Acts 17:18*) were the
prevailing philosophical schools in ancient Roman
Empire during Apostolic Church times. The Stoic
has been called the Pharisee of philosophy while the
Sadducee was it Epicurean. Epicureanism is a system
of philosophy based on the teachings of Epicurus, an
atomic materialist and was founded around 307 BCE.
Epicurus (341 – 270 BCE) was an ancient Greek
philosopher and founder of the school of

Epicureanism. His materialism path led him to attack superstition and divine intervention and to the idea that pleasure was the greatest good. He counted the purpose of philosophy was to attain a happy life through a simple tranquil life characterized by peace and the absence of pain. He taught that pain and pleasure are measures of good and evil, that death is the end of the body and soul and is not to be feared. He also taught that gods do not punish, the universe is infinite and eternal and that events are based on motions and interaction of moving atoms in empty spaces.

Stoicism is a school of Hellenistic philosophy founded in Athens by Zeno of Citium.in the early 3rd century. The Stoics taught that destructive emotions resulted from errors in judgment and that a sage or person of moral and intellectual perfection would not suffer such emotions. They taught that virtue is sufficient for happiness. They were concerned with relationship between the cosmic connections and human freedom. They advocated the brotherhood of humanity and the equality of mankind and were noted for their stand on clemency concerning slaves. Stoicism equates God with the totality of the universe, and unlike Christianity, does not tell of a beginning or end nor does it say that an individual has an afterlife.

THE DOCTRINE OF THE BAPTISMAL SACRAMENT

This *dogma* or doctrine of the baptismal sacrament describes the practice and role of baptism during the early church:

How was baptism viewed by some of the church leaders and theologians included below?

(1) Ignatius – St Ignatius of Antioch, who is also called Prochorus, wrote an epistle to Church of God the Father and of Jesus Christ in Smyrna which is in Asia. His home of Antioch is the place where believers were first called Christians (*Acts 11:26*); a haven of persecuted Christians (*Acts 11:19*); and home of the first Gentile Church); as well as other honorable mentions... It was also one of the seven churches in Revelation in which Jesus said in part I know thy works, and tribulation, and poverty but thou art rich… *Revelation 2:9* gives added insight to the zeal of St Ignatius of Antioch.   Baptism, as one of the two ordinances established by Jesus for the church was addressed by Ignatius in an epistle to

Polycarp, Bishop of the Church of the Smyrmaens. He wished them much joy in the blameless spirit and the word of God and cited ordinances and statutes of God among which was the warning against division and unlawful baptism. He regarded the bishop's consent for baptism as well pleasing to God.

(2) Didache (teaching) - The Teaching of the Twelve Apostles is a brief early Christian treatise, dated to the late first or early second century. Parts of the text constitute the oldest surviving written catechism, has three main sections dealing with Christian ethics, rituals such as baptism and the Eucharist, and Church organization. It is considered the first example of the genre of the Church Order. Their view concerning the Neophytes or new converts involved the preparatory work of baptism, regular fasting and at least three daily prayers. They also listed different ways to rehearse baptisms, the different sources of water, the water temperature, and the different means of administering the water, as well as the necessary people to be involved.

(3) Justin Martyr (AD 100-ca165) was born in modern-day West Bank and is considered to be the first Apologist – a religious discipline in defense of

religious doctrine through argumentation. Only two of his apologies and one dialogue survive. He is regarded as the foremost interpreter of the theory of the Logos in the 2nd century. He says this washing or baptism is called illumination because they who learn these things are illuminated in their understanding. They understand that in the name of Jesus Christ who was crucified under Pontius Pilate and the Holy Ghost who foretold these things through the prophets is Himself the Illuminator.

(4) *Tertullian* (c.160 – c.225 AD), was a prolific early Christian writer from Carthage in the Roman Empire. His name was anglicized. He too was an Apologist. His view on baptism is that the sacrament of water by washing away the sins of early blindness, we are set free and admitted to eternity. He admonishes against the venomous Kainite doctrine to destroy baptism. He espouses the fact that the very simplicity of God means of working serves as a stumbling block to the carnal mind.

(5) *Hippolytus of Rome* (170 – 235) was the most important 3rd century theologian in the Christian Church in Rome where he is thought to be born. He is said to be a disciple of Irenaeus who was said to be

a disciple of Polycarp. He came into conflict with
the pope of his time. He was highly resistant to new
innovations of his "former" friends. He questioned
new converts about their hearing, life, occupation
and every thing that appertained to them and in the
end, he advocated that one had to be chosen to be
baptized.

(6) John Chrysostom (c.347 – c.407), Archbishop
of Constantinople, was another early Church Father.
He was known for his eloquence in preaching and
public speaking, and his denunciation of abuse of
authority by ecclesiastical and political leaders. His
baptismal stance is that of lauding the initiation into
the kingdom, enumeration of the valued gifts they are
endowed with from the Bridegroom, and the relation
to the converts the worthiness of serving God. He
is known for rendering 12 instruction to the
discourse to believers which tells them about the
laver, their illumination and it purpose of
regeneration and not of remission of sins.

FAITH AND THE CHURCH

The case for faith makes its case for witnessing from the Book Eight in reference to Augustine's conversion to Christ. In Chapter 1 he writes "Of a certainty, all men are vain who do not have the knowledge of God, or have not been able, from the good things that are seen, to find Him who is good. But I was no longer   fettered in that vanity. I had surmounted it, and from the united testimony of thy whole creation had found thee, our Creator, and thy Word – God with thee, and together with thee and the Holy Spirit, One God- by whom thou hast created all things.

The absolute and universal supremacy of God is affirmed in every aspect and dimension whether it is visible or invisible, thrones or dominions, powers or principalities. The case for faith is popularly found to be in Hebrews 11. We see that faith comes by hearing, and hearing by the word of God and that without faith it is impossible to please God: and he that cometh to God must first believe that He is, and that He is a rewarder of them that diligently seek Him. *Hebrews 11:1, 6*, We see that Christ Jesus was

faithful even unto the death on the cross. He bore
the cup of suffering even though He was the Creator
of all. By faith a man named Enoch was translated
right through death. By faith a man named Noah
became an heir of righteous along with his family.
By faith a man named Abraham, was called to go to a
place which he should afterward receive for an
inheritance, he obeyed not knowing the specifics. He
and all his heirs became inheritors. By faith Sara,
Abraham's wife, conceived seed that was delivered
out of season. By faith Abraham offered up Isaac,
his only begotten son, accounting God able to raise
him from the dead. By faith, Isaac blessed his sons
of things as yet unseen, Jacob blessed Joseph's sons
even as he was dying; Joseph gave commandment to
bring his bones to the yet unseen land; Moses passed
into the bushes, through the sea and over the wall;
the harlot Rahab received spies with peace; the
Israelites passed through the Red Sea on dry land;
and the walls of Jericho fell down after they were
compassed about seven days. Innumerable weakness
waxed valiant, kingdoms were subdued, resurrections
wrought, alien armies put to flight and by faith Jesus
Himself framed worlds by His Word. Time itself

would fail in order to tell of the many witnesses, having obtained a good report through faith not having received the promise. God provided a better thing so that all may be made perfect in one.

PLURALISM AND THE CHURCH

In an effort to minimize religious rivalry, pluralism emerged as a type of permissive agreement agreement.[10]   There is a seeking to cooperate or otherwise tolerate and respect the virtues of another's religion. Until those virtues are known by something or someone, their contents are empty and have no substance or real meaning. To know the One is to have the realistic view of that someone or that something. In Christ there is the following:

Christ is the One mediator between God and man.

Jesus is the one symbol of humanity's relationship to the transcendent God

Jesus' relationship is one with the Spirit that is the life-giving power of the Creator.

Jesus inaugurated the eschatological age of healing and hope and affected a new relationship between God and humanity.

The revelational presence of God was in Christ Jesus as the medium through which God is made known.

THE DOCTRINE OF ESCHATOLOGY:
The Last Things- The Christian Hope

Hence, we go to the last Book of the Bible itself for the eschatological dimensions of the Christian doctrine of salvation. Revelation of St. John the Divine is the last book in the New Testament. It cites the struggle between good and evil and the triumphant outcome of Christ and His church. Revelation in Greek is the word *apokalupsis,* which means to unveil or uncover. In regards to its use in writing it means to reveal or make clear. When used in regards to a person it denotes a visible presence. When used in connection with Jesus Christ it refers to both the book or writing and the person of Jesus Christ (*Ephesians 3:3; Galatians 1:12; 2Thessolonians 1:7 1 Peter 1:7, 13*). It is both a revelation concerning Jesus as well as a revelation from him. The central message therefore is the Revelation of Jesus Christ.

Revelation was written by John, the Apostle from the Greek Isle of Patmos, during the late first century... The narrative states that God gave the revelation to Jesus Christ, then Christ sent and signified it by his angel to John, and John bare record of the word of God, and of the testimony of Jesus Christ, and of all things that he saw *(Revelation 1:1)*. Jesus identifying Himself as the Alpha and Omega, the first and the last, told John to write what he had seen in a book and send it unto the seven churches which are in Asia. Thus the earthly setting (the heavenly setting being in the Spirit on the Lord's Day) [xiv] in which John resided is the locale of Asia Minor during the dispensation of the Church Age. The Book of Revelation is thought to coincide most likely with Emperor Domitian's reign in A.D. 81-96.

Additionally, the letters to the seven churches appear to be compatible with dates of Domitian's reign (pg 159). It was delivered to the seven local churches in the form of letters and portrayed actual conditions in Asia Minor along the western coast of Turkey. Prophetically the application speaks to the churches throughout this dispensation which includes this present modern-day society. The spiritual conditions are revealed in the local church as well as in the individuals who assemble therein. Hence, all generations are warned on the one hand and may profit by learning from the listed failures among the seven churches on the other hand...

The dispensational application espouses that the seven letters portray seven distinct church ages and seven distinct phases of church history though the age of grace is not clearly taught in the Book. Thereby much confusion and false teachings surround that theory. There is the school of thought that states that Christians and churches should apply all of the seven letters as we do all other New Testament Books wherein the aspects of all may be enjoyed. Christ Jesus speaks to the seven churches in a very precise order as follows:

First, Christ identifies Himself.

Then, He commends the church with the exception of Laodicea

Next, He condemns the things that are wrong with the exception of Smyrna and Philadelphia.

Then, He exhorts the church.

Finally, He challenges the church

To cite one example as given by Alan B. Stringfellow, we read the following: "Unto the pastor of the church of Ephesus write (This was the church of the Apostles. Note now the pattern of our Lord to Ephesus)

He identifies himself: 2:1 – "These things saith He that holdeth the seven stars in His right hand who walks in the midst of the seven golden candlesticks."

He commends the church: V-2-3, "I know thy works, thy labor, thy patience, etc,"

He reproves: V-4, "Nevertheless, I have somewhat against thee, because thou hast left thy first love."

He admonishes: V-5-6, "Remember – repent or I will remove the candlestick."

He challenges: V-7, "He that hath an ear, let him hear what the Spirit saith unto the churches; to him that overcometh will I give to eat of the tree of life which is in the midst of the paradise of God."

Revelation as prophecy from God contains three beatitudes. They are (1) Blessed is he that readeth it (2) and they that hear the words of this prophecy, and (3) and they that keep those things which are written therein. For the time is at hand (*Rev 1:3*). He that hath an ear, let him hear what the Spirit is saying to the churches. As overcomers. believers shall eat of the tree of life which is in the Paradise of God; shall not taste of the second death; shall eat of the hidden manna and receive a white stone with a new special name written on it; shall have authority and power over nations, shall be victorious ones clothed in garments of white, shall have their names written in the Lamb's Book of Life, and our Lord Jesus Christ shall confess our names before the Father. We are blessed to be made pillars in the temple, to apprehend that for which we have been apprehended-the name of God and the name of the city of God which is new Jerusalem, and Jesus' new name.

The structure in the Book of Revelation covers the spectrum of things that were seen, things which are, and things which shall be hereafter *(Revelation 1:4)*. John saw the vision of the glorified Christ, the seven churches, the vision of heaven and the Sovereign God seated on the throne being worshipped. He saw the sealed scrolls in God's hand, the Lamb that was slain before the foundation of the world, the seven seals as they were being opened, the twelve tribes of Israel that had been sealed and an innumerable multitude that had come out of great tribulation. He saw the silence in heaven, the seven trumpets, the cataclysmic disasters of hail and fire from heaven, a mountain cast into the sea, a great star falling from the sky, astronomical changes, destructive locusts, and a huge conquering army.

John saw a little scroll that he was instructed to eat, two witnesses who prophesy and are killed and raised again, the singing of hymns of praise to God for his triumph and his judgments. He saw seven significant signs or visions – a woman clothed with the sun, the moon under her feet, on her head a crown of twelve stars, being in labor and in pain. He saw a great red dragon having seven heads and ten horns on his head with seven diadem. He saw the great whore that sitteth upon many waters. He saw a woman set up upon a scarlet colored beast arrayed in purple and scarlet color, and decked in gold and precious stones and pearls, having a golden cup in her hand full of abominations and filthiness of her fornications. Upon her forehead was a name written Mystery, Babylon the Great, the Mother of Harlots and Abominations of the Earth.' Michael and his angels fighting a dragon (Satan) who is cast out of heaven and fights the woman and her son on earth. He saw the world worshipping a beast out of the sea, the beast that comes out of the earth and dominates the world. There were 144,000 tribesmen of Israel praising the Lamb. One "like a son of man" harvested the earth. Seven bowls held the last plagues. The triumphant tribulationists who overcame the beast were praising God. The angels came out of the temple with bowls of plagues that were poured out successively upon the earth rendering painful sores for those with the mark of the beast and had worshiped his image. The sea, the rivers and springs turned into blood. The heat from the sun was scorching hot. The Euphrates River dried. Evil spirits ascended from the abyss. The nations gathered for the battle at Armageddon. He saw the climax of utter earthly destruction.

John sees the triumph of the Almighty God in the world and the world to come. The wicked are judged and the righteous are rewarded. God condemns and destroys *Mystery Babylon* which represents the evil and ungodly suppressor of God's people and those who profited from her must now mourn. A great multitude of invitees share in the wedding supper of the Lamb, praising God, for the rider on the white horse has defeated the beasts and the assembled nations. John describes the "thousand years" (or "millennium"), Satan is bound, and "the first resurrection occurs. He sees Satan lead the final rebellion and God destroys him. God judges all the dead before the great white throne judgment –the second resurrection, - the first earth passes away and there is a new heaven and a new earth in which God resides with his people. He sees the righteous separated from the wicked and the New Jerusalem; the "bride, the wife of the Lamb" in the image of a New Jerusalem whose features and dimensions are described in full detail.

There was no temple nor sun nor moon in this city. God and the Lamb lived there and are the light of it. Wickedness did not exist there. He remembers the prophesy that Jesus said concerning his promise to come again soon. *(Revelation 4:1 -22:18}* (Pgs156-158)2. The message John saw was and is trustworthy and reliable (*Revelation 22:19-21*): There are varying interpretations of this book and briefly stated they are as follows:

(1) The Preterist Interpretation is the belief that Revelation has already been fulfilled in the years and generation of the past.

(2) *Historically Continuous Interpretation* is the belief that Revelation is a panorama of the history of the church from the days of John

(3) *The Spiritualizers or Idealists* interpret the Book as a symbol of the great struggle between good and evil. They regard the Book of Revelation as being symbolic only and not actual.

(4) *The Futurist Interpretation* holds the belief that the beginning of the fourth Chapter of Revelation (the things that shall be hereafter) is an unveiling of the consummation of the age and is vividly described and or depicted in the ensuing chapters up through *Revelation 19:7.*

The Book of Revelation is a tremendous contribution to understanding faith via the following:

(1) *Use of Old Testament*: Revelation contains the most quoted Old Testament Scriptures, more than any other NT book whether alliterative or conceptual.

(2) *God's Sovereignty*: Envisioning God being worshipped on his throne keeps us reminded of the praise and devotion that is due Him.

(3) Christ's Preeminence. Jesus is constantly and significantly portrayed in accomplishing the purposes of God the Father on earth.

(4) Christ's Cross. The cross is to be kept at the forefront for there he shed His precious, innocent blood and died a sacrificial death that we may have life. Yet rejoicing in his resurrection, ascension, glory, power and role in judgment which is his due also.

(5) End of History:

Future events. The eschatological interests are richly served through the detailed descriptions provided in the Book of Revelation.

Present -day living. Knowing the end from the beginning helps to enlighten our understanding of where we fit in. It also exhorts or warns of the reality and severity of our actions.

God's judgment. There is a great recompense of reward for trusting and believing in Jesus Christ as our Lord and Savior. There is also a day of wrath for the unbeliever. We have hope and a great comfort because of the vision given to Jesus Christ who sent his angel to John that he might show to his servants the things that must come.

CONCLUSION

In conclusion the report of the Author is one of hope and assurance of the outcome of the covenantal relationship to believers as declared and decreed in His Word. It is about the triumph of Jesus Christ having come into the world on behalf of men for the salvation and redemption of their souls and to restore them to the personal apprehension of relationship with the Living Savior. Jesus Christ died for our sins according to scripture; was buried, and rose again the third day according to scripture. Lord Jesus Christ is One mind and there is no conceivable opponent.

The God of Scripture is the God of the Word. Everything is working at the Maker's bidding. Not a hair of the head can be touched without God's allowance or permission. A man's heart devises his way: but the LORD directs his steps. What assurance, what faithfulness, what strength, what comfort He affords to those who come to Him as well as those who do not. We have a more sure word of prophecy – the word as it is written. One can rest in the LORD for He is a faithful King. He has given to humankind the way of love and righteousness wherein *knowing the Truth* one is liberated. He has *given* the gift of eternal life that we may *know* Him. The exploration and explanation of the revelation is that He has chosen *you* that you should *know* his will, and see that Just One, and should hear the voice of his mouth in order to be a witness in the earth. He appears through the hearing of His voice, the reading of His Word, the speaking of the written word or any and every communique which are all available to Him. Again, to know the One is to have the realistic view of that someone or that something. In the case of Jesus Christ there is the following:

(1) Christ is the One mediator

(2) Jesus is the One symbol of humanity's relationship to the transcendent God

(3) Jesus' relationship is one with the Spirit that is the life-giving power of the Creator.

(4) Jesus inaugurated the eschatological age of healing and hope as well as the last things and affected a new relationship between God and humanity.

M. Helen Ingram

(5) The revelational presence of God was in
     Christ Jesus as the medium through which
     God is made *known*.

*"SchemA Israel, Hear of Israel, the Lord our God is One. "It Takes
One to Know One."*

ENDNOTES

[i]HTTP://EN.WIKIPEDIA.ORG//WIKI/CHRISTOLOGY
     [ii] ETHELBERT W. BULLINGER, NUMBER IN
SCRIPTURE (LONDON: EYRE AND SPOTTISWOODE,
1894) KINDLE EBOOK
          5 HTTP://WWW.HCCENTRAL.COM/DGOD.HTML[iii]
          [iv]ETHELBERT W. BULLINGER, NUMBER IN
SCRIPTURE (LONDON: EYRE AND SPOTTISWOODE, 1894)
KINDLE E-BOOK
          [v]

HTTP://EN.WIKIPEDIA.ORG/WIKI/CHRISTOLOGY
          [vi] ALISTER E. MCGRATH, CHRISTIAN THEOLOGY:
AN INTRODUCTION (KINGS COLLEGE: BLACKWELL
PUBLISHING, 2011)
          [vii] HTTP://WWW/HCCENTRAL.COM/DGOD.HTML
          [viii] MCGRATH, 280-1
          [ix]HTTP://ECBRAGG.NET/CLASS%20NOTES/SOTER
IOLOGY. HTM
          [x] THOMAS D. LEA & DAVID ALAN BLACK, THE

NEW TESTAMENT: ITS BACKGROUND AND MESSAGE
(NASHVILLE: B & H PUBLISHING, 2003)
> [xi] LEA & BLACK, 289
> [xii] LEA & BLACK, 292
> [xiii] LEA & BLACK, 294

D.A. CARSON AND DOUGLAS J MOO, INTRODUCING THE
NEW TESTAMENT: A GUIDE TO ITS HISTORY AND
MESSAGE, GRAND RAPIDS: ZONDERVAN, 2010

DICTIONARY OF THEOLOGICAL TERMS

(1) *Biblical theology* – A branch of theology that describes spiritual doctrines in context with the individual writer's concepts.

(2) *Systematic theology* – A branch of theology that connects a series of doctrines to a system. The attempt is to show the connection of all doctrines as a consistent whole.

(3) *Agnostic* – A Greek term that literally means unknown, without knowledge, ignorant.

(4) *Godhead* – The term signifies the Divinity and unity of the Father, Son, and Holy Spirit. It is synonymous with the term Trinity.

(5) *Eternal security* – This doctrine teaches that an individual cannot do anything that could revoke their salvation

(6) *Humanism* – It is a faith in the goodness of man and a confidence that he can resolve all issues without any need for a God.

(7) *Eschatology* – The section of theology that deals with the last things. It describes the issues of end time prophesy, such as, millennium, the tribulation, the second coming of Christ

(8) *Soteriology* – The section of Christian theology dealing with the doctrine of salvation.

(9) *Christology* – The theology dealing with the identity of Jesus Christ, particularly the question of the relation of his human and divine natures

(10.) *Sovereignty* – The most exalted of its kind

(11) *Pluralism* – The religious definition is the belief that one can overcome religious differences between different religions and denominational conflicts within the same religion.

(12) *Revelation* – Theologically it is communication, by a divinity or by divine agency, of divine truth or knowledge; specifically, God's manifestation of the divinity or of the divine will to humanity

BIBLIOGRAPHY

Bullinger, Ethelbert W. Number in Scripture: The Supernatural Design and Spiritual Significance. London: Eyre and Spottiswoode, 1894.

Carson, D.A. and Moo, Douglas. Introducing the New Testament: A Short Guide in its History and Message. Grand Rapids: Zondervan Publishing Co. 2010.

Conner, Kevin J. and Malmin, Ken. Interpreting the Scriptures: A Textbook on How to Interpret the Bible. Oregon: City Publishing, 1983.

Deere, John. Surprised by the Voice of God: How God Speaks Today Through Prophecies, Dreams, and Visions. Grand Rapids: Zondervan Publishing House.

Dake, Finis Jennings. Dake's Annotated Reference Bible. Lawrenceville: Dake Publishing Inc., 1999.

King James Version of the Holy Bible. Nashville: Broadman & Holman Publishers

Lea, Thomas D. and Black, David Alan. The New Testament: Its Background and Message. Nashville: B. & H. Publishing Group, 2003.

Harnack, Adolph von. History of Dogma. New York: Dover
Publications, 1961.

McGrath, Alister E. Christian Theology: An Introduction.
Kings College: Blackwell Publishing, 2011.

Miller, Madeleine S. and Miller, J. Lane. Harper's Bible
Dictionary. New York: Harper & Row. 1961.

Minns, Denis. Iranaeus: An Introduction/Denis Minns.
London: New York: T & T Clark, c2010

Packer, James Innell.Knowing God. Downers Grove:
Intervarsity Press, 1973.

Pink, Arthur Walkington. The Attributes of God. Grand
Raoids: Baker Books, 2006

Prothero, Stephen R. God is Not One: The Eight Rival
Religions That Run The World-And Why Their Differences
Matter. New York: Harper One c2010.

Richardson, Alan and Bowden, John. The Westminster
Dictionary of Christian Theology. Philadelphia: The
Westminster Press, 1983.

Shelley, Bruce. Historical Theology. An Introduction to Christian Doctrine: A Companion to Wayne Gruden's Systematic Theology. Grand Rapids: Zondervan, c2011

Stringfellow, Dr, Akan B. Through the Bible in One Year. Tulsa: Hensley Publishing, 1998.

Strobel, Lee. The Case For Faith: A Journal Investigates the Toughest Objections to Christianity. Grand Rapids: Zondervan, 1998.

Strobel, Lee. The Case For Christ: A Journalist's Personal Investigation of the Evidence for Jesus. Grand Rapids:

Tozier, Arden Wilson. The Knowledge of the Holy. New York: HarperCollins Publishers, 1961.

http://en.wikipedia.org/wiki/Christology.

http://en.wikipedia.org/wiki/Salvation_(Christianity)

http:www.earlychristianwriting.com/text/justinmartyr-firstapology.html.

http://www.learnthebible.org/outline-for-the-doctrine-of-gpd.htm

http://www.hccentral.com/dgod.htmo

http:www.crossroad.to/HisWord/verses/topics/kniwubg-God.htm

http://www.ucg.org/booklet/god-trinity/how-god-one/

http://www.gotquestions.org/knowing-God.html

http://em.widipedia.org/wiki/Church Fathers

http://ecbragg.net/Class%20Notes/Soteriology.htm

http://www.wordig.com/definition/Religious_[;ira;os,

http://www.sounddoctrine.net/Bible/Soteriology_<irre;;.htm

M. Helen Ingram

About The Author

M. Helen Ingram is a proud mother, blessed grandmother, teacher, church elder, and poetic tour-de- force is a graduate of Shaw University. Recently, she received her Masters of Divinity from The Sword Of The Spirit Bible Institute. She resides near Washington, DC, where she loves to garden and spend time with her loving children, grandchildren, and great childre

It Takes One To Know One

M. Helen Ingram

Other Titles By Author...

God Think! Ruminations of A Child Of God Volume I
God Think! Ruminations of A Child Of God Volume II
Sharecropper's Grand

It Takes One To Know One

Beloved Husband, George Ingram, Sr.

George, Jr. (son), Earl Ingram (grandson), Eric Ingram (son), Timothy Ingram (grandson), Anthony Ingram (great-grandson), Bill Ingram (son)

Timothy Ingram (grandson), Nicolle Ingram (granddaughter), Bill Ingram (son), George Jr.(son), Cheryl Ingram (daughter), Ashleigh Ingram (granddaughter), Kayleigh Ingram (great-granddaughter), Anthony Ingram (great-grandson), Earl Ingram (grandson)

Erica Ingram (great-granddaughter)

Eric Ingram and wife, Wendy Ingram

Eric Ingram adopting Wendy's son, Jamez Ingram